Words Bottled UP

Poems, thoughts and more...

Sneha Pai
'Nikki'

BlueRose ONE
Stories Matter

First Published in July 2022

ISBN: 978-93-5628-505-7

BLUEROSE PUBLISHERS

www.BlueRoseONE.com

info@bluerosepublishers.com

+91 8882 898 898

Cover Design:

Aveek

Typographic Design:

Rohit

Distributed by: BlueRose, Amazon, Flipkart

Dedicated to

My wonderful family and friends who have been the anchor of my life.

Contents

Introduction

"Poetry is when an emotion has found its thought and the thought has found words." – Robert Frost

In a day, a thousand thoughts run through our minds. Family, friends, work, love, life, past, future, movies, sports — the chain of thoughts is endless.

In some minds these thoughts occupy more space,
All the words somehow fall in place,
Creating beautiful lines of poetry,
What is in the mind, is now for the world to see.

Dear reader,

I am Sneha Pai, also known by my pen name 'Nikki', and *words bottled up* is a collection of poems and quotes that I have written over the years. I used to be an overthinker, flooded by thoughts one after the other. The thoughts that were in my mind one night started making sense and my first poem "Love inspires" was born. It was as though the thoughts and the words that were bottled up were coming out as poetry, hence the name. And this was just the beginning. Soon, I had written poems for most of the aspects of my life. All my emotions were out there as poetry. I started observing more of the environment we are surrounded by, about the people around me; people who were enjoying their lives, people who were heartbroken, and all of this inspired me to write about all kinds of emotions.

Based on the different topics, the poems have been categorised into sections for **life**, **inspiration**, **love**, **broken heart**, **it's all about me**, and **our world**. There are some wonderful quotes by wise individuals in each of the sections that have been added to the book to remind us that these thoughts and words are available to us from hundreds of years. We only need to give these thoughts a little attention.

I hope these poems and quotes resonate with you and help you learn and understand the emotions we feel at different times in life.

Happy reading!

Life

"Life isn't about finding yourself,
Life is about creating yourself."

George Bernard Shaw

"The future depends on what we do in the present."

Mahatma Gandhi

"The two most important days in your life are the day you are born and the day you find out why."

Mark Twain

"You will face many defeats in life, but never let yourself be defeated."

Maya Angelou

What is life?

Life is a journey. For some, it's a gift, a mystery, a celebration, and for others, life is tough, frustrating, stressful.

Life can have different meanings to different people, and it can be different to the same people in different phases of their life. Where we are in our life right now is what best defines life for us.

Life goes on

Friends depart on a sad note,
Moving away, differing with each other, a misquote,
Changing the bond created thereupon,
Life changes, but it goes on...

Loved ones hurting one another,
Egos clashing, trying hard to be together,
Being in a relation where you don't belong,
Sadly, life goes on...

Tired souls coping with life,
Trying hard keeping alive,
Facing problems, pretending to be strong,
Despite all this, life goes on...

Change the way you see things,
Enjoy every moment, talk about your feelings,
Choose to be happy, smile all along,
Whatever happens, life goes on...

"In three words I can sum up everything I've learned about life: it goes on."

– Robert Frost

Live life today

Smile, make others smile with you,
Hug, convey your feelings through,
Laugh, let it enhance the way you feel,
Cry when you want to, it's no big deal,
Kiss deeply, stop the time,
Breathe and you know everything is fine,
Listen to your heartbeat, feel secure,
Fall in love like never before,
Do what you can, expect nothing,
Live the moment, capture everything,
Forget tomorrow, let go yesterday,
All we need to do is live life today.

"You only live once, but if you do it right, once is enough."
– Mae West

What do you want from life?

If you want a life full of love,
You must be ready to open your hearts now,
Give love to everyone around,
For love comes back to you plentiful and abound.

If you want a life full of prosperity,
You must have a heart full of generosity,
It means you have more than enough when you give,
A sense of gratitude for all that you have received.

If you want a life full of health,
You must first understand that health is wealth,
Work towards being better than what you are today,
Step by step, you'll be there one day.

Whatever you want from life, just give,
Spread some love, willingly forgive,
For then you'll find an inner peace,
To allow and create for yourself a life of bliss.

"Only by giving are you able to receive more than you already have."

– Jim Rohn

Life, make it beautiful

There are days when you feel everything is going wrong,
Hold on, don't despair, make your mind strong,
There are people around, trying to pull you down all the time,
Don't listen, they are not worth a dime,
There are moments when you get discouraged by criticism,
Handle it, don't worry about the outcome.

When all the negativity of life stifles you,
Take a deep breath and think of the one's who love you,
It's never easy to let go of the thoughts that bother,
But now is the time to rise above and emerge stronger,
Block out the unpleasantness, focus on everything that's wonderful,
Keep telling yourself that life can only be beautiful.

"Very little is needed to make a happy life; it is all within yourself, in your way of thinking."
– Marcus Aurelius

Is life an illusion?

Emotions are transitory, mind fleeting,
The world that we live in is make believe; devoid of real feelings,
We hope that things around are as we see,
But the reality is different from our perspective, making us want to flee,
Happiness, sorrow, anger, fear are all momentary,
Feelings vanish even before we can revel in it completely,
Forging us to think on our very being; our creation,
Making us wonder, is life just an illusion?

"We live in a fantasy world, a world of illusion. The great task in life is to find reality."

– Iris Murdoch

What is life?

Life is a crazy ride,
Let's enjoy, have fun, instead of being petrified,
Life is a pain,
Let's have patience, since time always doesn't remain same,
Life is a dream,
Let's work hard, realize the unseen,
Life is simple,
Let's quit worrying and trust our impulse,
Life is tough,
Let's jump the hurdles, instead of creating a fuss,
Life is love,
It'll be ours if we believe in it enough,
Life is beautiful,
Let's live in happiness and make it blissful.

"Life is a journey, not a destination."
– Ralph Waldo Emerson

"I slept and dreamt that life was joy. I awoke and saw that life was service. I acted and behold, service was joy."
– Rabindranath Tagore

Life is short

We think we have all the time,
To create memories that will last a lifetime,
Holding onto things and not letting them go,
Living with our ego, is what we know.
Anger, blame, resentment, breaks what we have made
Regrets will remain and leave us frayed,
Live the moment and create a new plan,
Life is short, so let's smile when we can.

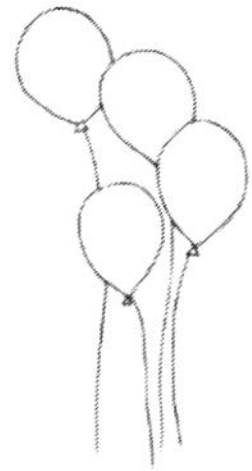

"*We live but for a moment.*"
– Marcus Aurelius

Live, laugh, love

Live life as if it's your last day,
You get to live once and there's no replay,
Listen to your heart, it's always right,
Do what you believe in, though it might give you a fright,
Make every day count, don't always blame it on fate,
Say what you feel, it's never too late,
Have fun, dance in the rain,
Laugh when you can, the moment might never come again,
Enjoy life today, go with the flow,
Love passionately as if there is no tomorrow,
Live without inhibitions, be kind, be true,
Life is a gift, laugh often, live well and love what
you do.

"Learn from yesterday, live for today, hope for tomorrow. The important thing is not to stop questioning."
– Albert Einstein

"Live every moment, Laugh every day, Love beyond words."
– Anonymous

Life is beautiful

Life is beautiful…

Be grateful,
Remain hopeful,
Act graceful,
Feel joyful,
Think useful,
Become successful,
Stay truthful,
Live blissful.

"Give every day the chance to become the most beautiful day of your life".

– Mark Twain

Inspiration

"Whatever you are, be a good one."
Abraham Lincoln

"You do not find the happy life. You make it."
Camilla Eyring Kimball

"Out of mountain of despair, a stone of hope."
Martin Luther King Jr.

"The greatest glory in living lies not in never falling but in rising every time we fall."
Nelson Mandela

"It is never too late to be who you might have been."
George Elliot

We all have developed different mindsets in our life based on what we have seen and heard and absorbed throughout our lives. At some point, we feel the need to have something more, to feel better, to awaken our sleeping minds. This is where inspiration helps. It makes us think, motivates us to take the next step and bring a positive outlook to our lives.

Follow your dreams

Everyone who exists, has a dream,
To achieve something that's unseen,
Knowingly, unknowingly, we all want something,
Motivating us to move forward and give our existence a new meaning.

A peaceful living, a work that we love,
A loving family to go home to,
A beautiful house, money to spend,
A lifetime of happiness and amazing friends.

Dreams give us a purpose to live,
A sense of direction to what we want to achieve,
Listen to your inner voice, have belief in your ability,
Follow your dreams and turn them into reality.

"Dream is not that which you see while sleeping it is something that does not let you sleep."

– Abdul Kalam

You can

When you feel tired and want to give up,
You keep walking when you just want to stop,
Smiling at people; concealing the screams,
Dark long nights and the endless dreams,
Moments slipping through your fingers like quicksand,
Everything is beyond what you can withstand,
Take a step back, pause a while,
Think about everything that made you smile,
Reflect your hope, believe in you,
What you make of your life, solely depends on you,
Give it a push, give it everything,
Trust yourself, YOU CAN do anything.

"Whether you can or you can't, you're right."
– Henry Ford

"Believe you can and you're halfway there."
– Theodore Roosevelt

Look inside you

How often do we judge others without understanding them,
Jumping to conclusions, ready to condemn,
Creating an opinion based on our perception,
When it might just be a figment of our imagination.

No one is perfect; no one has it easy,
Everyone is going through their own fight individually,
Before you judge others, pause,
Don't create a story that never was.

People are the way they are for a reason,
Circumstances, experience, is what makes a person,
We are not walking their journey, so stop criticizing,
Let people live the way they have been living.

Find your flaws first, own your action,
Spend more time evolving your own passion,
Before judging others, look inside you,
In life, there are always better things to do.

"When you judge another, you do not define them, you define yourself."

- Dr. Wayne Dyer

Feelings

Feelings within defines us,
Some we hide, some we show, some we are scared to touch,
Driving us to take decisions that's not always right,
Holding onto our emotions with all our might,
Giving up, when it's time to rise,
Doubting ourselves despite the highs,
Creating a world of our own,
Fearing to venture outside of our comfort zone,
Feelings freak us out, but they also help us grow,
Hoping for better things, waiting for tomorrow,
Celebrating moments with happiness,
Embracing failures and success,
Not knowing what the future holds for us,
Trusting our feelings is what life is all about.

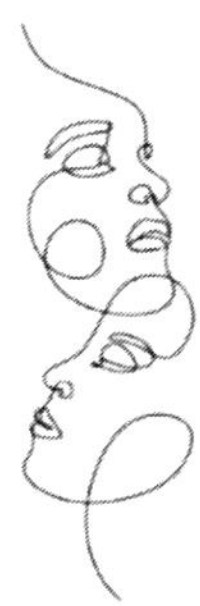

"Our feelings are our most genuine paths to knowledge."
- Audre Lorde

Voices within us

The happy voices within me singing my favourite song,
The sound of rains in tune with the song,
I notice every small thing, I smile at everyone I see,
Where there's happiness, there's a sense of being free.

The sad voices crying within me filling me with elancholy,
The rains in agreement drenching me completely,
I don't want to look at anything, I don't want
anyone to know,
Where there's sadness, there's depression, there's woe.

The angry voices within me wanting to come out screaming,
The rains syncing with my anger with thunder and lightning,
I hide my turbulence with a smile that is forced,
Where there's anger, there's a rage that is about to burst.

The voices within us that we keep hearing,
Reveal our inner most feelings,
Listen to the voices, take time to think,
How we tackle the voices is what makes us distinct.

"The more faithfully you listen to the voices within you, the better you will hear what is sounding outside."

– Dag Hammarskjöld

Let it go

Hurt feelings, stifled cries,
Emotions galore, trying to hide,
Troubled relationship, ready to break,
Disturbed dreams keeping you awake,
Carrying on, despite the low,
Don't hold on, let it go...

Stressed life, lots to prove,
Wary of race, always on the move,
Fighting for attention, waiting for the perk,
Doing what you don't like, to rise at work,
Losing self just to grow,
For a peaceful life, let it go...

Reliving bygones, stuck in past,
Working for tomorrow, today is lost,
Struggling to balance everything you care for,
Eluding happiness in pursuit of something more,
Instead do what you love, learn to say no,
Though it's not easy, let it go...

"Some of us think holding on makes us strong; but sometimes it is letting go."

– Herman Hesse

Move on

There are moments in our life that inspire us beyond compare,
Unexpected feelings that create turmoil to give us a scare,
Events that we want to erase and forget,
Things we've done that has left us with regret,
Magical emotions that make us believe in love,
Sweet memories that we can't let go of,
Every experience good or bad is past, it's already gone,
It's time to enjoy the now and just move on.

"Life moves on and so should we."
– Spencer Johnson

"I walk slowly but I never walk backward."
– Abraham Lincoln

Keep smiling

Smile often,
Whether or not you are having fun,
Smile when you feel like,
Doesn't matter what others think, it's alright,
Smile when you feel sad,
Half your problems will not seem as bad,
Smile at strangers,
When you smile, they might forget their tears,
Smile thinking of people you love,
You can achieve everything you dream of,
You have one life, so quit thinking,
Whatever life throws at you, keep smiling.

"Let us always meet each other with a smile, for smile is the beginning of love."

– Mother Teresa

Emotions

There are so many emotions within,
Conversing and creating conflicts,
Generating thoughts faster than what the mind can process,
A sense of turmoil that is difficult to express,
Feelings that transpose abruptly,
Forming impressions that is not visible clearly,
How do you manage the restlessness that refuses to cease?
When all you want in life is some inner peace.

"Emotion can be the enemy. If you give into your emotion, you lose yourself. You must be at one with your emotions, because the body always follow the mind."

– Bruce Lee

Why, oh why?

Why does every small thing affect us often?
Why do we allow people to control our emotions?
Why do we get impacted by the external noise?
Why do we let negative events disturb our poise?

Life teaches us not to expect anything,
But with all our hope, we just cling,
Why, oh why, do we look at the outer world for our dreams?
When all what we want is embedded within.

"If everything around you seems dark, look again, you may be the light."

– Rumi

Thoughts

Put your confused thoughts to sleep,
they are useless anyway,
Kill the sinful thoughts for good,
they'll take your peace away,
Erase the painful thoughts
that moisten your eyes,
Nurture the positive thoughts,
only those will get you through your life.

"A man is but the product of his thoughts; what he thinks he becomes."

– Mahatma Gandhi

"Change your thoughts and you change your world."

– Norman Vincent Peale

Do it

Acknowledge,
Someone's mood may just get better,
Compliment,
Someone's life may get a bit sweeter,
Appreciate,
Someone's efforts may feel valued,
Converse,
Someone's perspective may get changed,
Respond,
Someone's day may depend on it,
Smile,
Someone's happiness may get a lift.

"There is no exercise better for the heart than reaching down and lifting people up."

– John Holmes

Go for what you want

There are more than enough reasons to smile,
You just have to open your mind for a while,
To notice all the good things that are out there,
It can all be yours if you care.

You must realise what you want in life,
Health, wealth, happiness, love, whatever makes you feel alive,
When you go after things that you really love,
It'll be yours and you'll figure out the how.

Take the first step and make a start,
Go for what you want with all your heart!

"Find purpose. The means will follow."
– Mahatma Gandhi

Love

"Where there is love, there is life."

Mahatma Gandhi

"There is only one happiness in this life, to love and be loved."

George Sand

"Love is composed of a single soul inhabiting two bodies."

Aristotle

"Love is the ultimate meaning of everything around us. It is not a mere statement. It is truth; it is the joy that is at the root of all creation."

Rabindranath Tagore

"Love opens the most impossible gates; love is the gate to all the secrets of the universe."

Swami Vivekananda

Love is an emotion that drives us. Love for our parents, partners, children, friends, pets, love for wealth, love for music – it's what makes us look forward to the days of our life. To have a heart full of love, to give love and graciously accept all the love we receive, is what gives us an inner gratification, a sense of belonging and fulfillment.

"Love is the humblest yet the most powerful force that the human being has."

- Mahatma Gandhi

Love inspires

You made me fall in love with you,
You made me feel for you,
Having now found love so true,
My feelings are all that I have for you.

I close my eyes, I see you,
In my dreams, I feel you,
Every moment, I think of you,
My heart, my mind, is so full of you.

They say, love is happiness,
Love makes you insane,
If this is what true love is,
I want to fall in love with you again and again.

There are ways to be inspired
And it's never easy,
But falling in love with the right person,
Makes you believe in yourself and feel for everything so deeply.

Love is beautiful, and so are you,
All I want you to say is, I love you!

"I love you for all that you are, all that you have been, and all you're yet to be."

– Ernest Hemingway

Love

Love is a powerful emotion
that can make anyone strong, or leave them broken,
With loves comes great responsibility
to always be there beyond infinity,
And it's not just words of love that sees it through,
there needs to be care, respect and understanding in
everything we do,
So, when you declare your love, be very sure,
else when the heart breaks there might be no cure,
The world is already full of fear, hatred, distrust now,
You wouldn't want one more person to stop
believing in love.

"Love is a combination of care, commitment, knowledge, responsibility, respect and trust."

- Bell Hooks

You

You are my inspiration,
When I let myself down, your belief in me is beyond imagination,
You are my strength,
When I feel like giving up, you manage to uplift me in the end
You are my laughter,
When I feel low, that's all that matters,
You are my soul,
When I feel incomplete, you make me feel whole,
You are my dream,
When I wake up with you, everything is peaceful and serene,
You are my life,
When there's darkness around, you are my sunshine.

"I love you not because of who you are, but because of who I am when I am with you."

– Roy Croft

Just be there

I know I am not perfect,
I am real, I make mistakes,
I might mess up everything, everywhere,
Whatever I do, just be there...

I get scared, I am alone,
I manage to pretend I am strong,
What I really want is to be cared,
When I look for you, just be there...

I feel confused, unable to take decisions,
I cry for every small reason,
I know I am sometimes difficult to bear,
However I am, just be there...

I long for a life filled with happiness,
It's tough for me to deal with stress,
I might stumble, totally unaware,
I will need you, just be there...

"Your presence is the most precious gift you can give to another human being."

– Marshall B Rosenberg

Be with me forever

You are the one in my prayers,
I want you to only smile, no tears,
You are the one in my dreams,
Just you and me, nothing in between,
You are the one in my thoughts,
Giving me directions, without you I am lost,
You are the one my heart wants,
Never have I felt feelings this strong,
You are the one who is a part my life,
I see you everywhere, even when I close my eyes,
You are the one I love,
With you, I feel a connection so true,
You are the one I treasure,
Regardless of where time takes us, be with me forever.

"True love is eternal, infinite, and always like itself."
– Honore de Balzac

It's all about love

Love the feeling of being with you,
How the time flies I hardly know,
Love the way you look at me with so much care,
It makes me feel special and rare,
Love it when you make me laugh and smile,
The tears of happiness make it all worthwhile,
Love the passion I see in your eyes,
Each day with you throws a new surprise,
Love every moment we are together,
I want to hold these moments within me forever.
Love is a wonderful emotion that makes me shine,
I know I am in love; I am feeling all the signs.

"The only thing we never get enough of is love; and the only thing we never give enough of is love."

– Henry Miller

Be the one

Be the hands that wipe my tears,
Be the courage to overcome my fears,
Be the arms that support when I fall,
Be the strength to endure it all,
Be the sunshine in the shade,
Be the glow on my face,
Be the smile on my lips,
Be the happiness I cannot miss,
Be the sparkle in my eyes,
Be the heartbeat of my life.

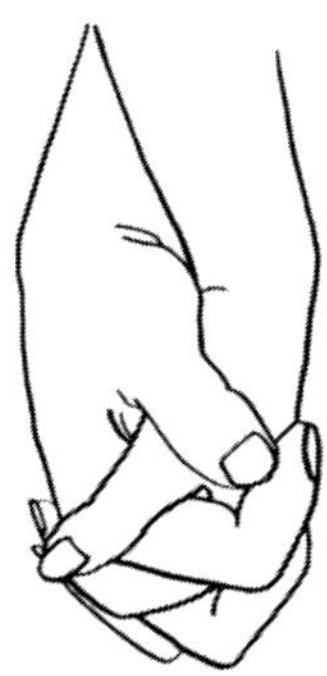

"When you love someone, the best thing you can offer is your presence. How can you love if you are not there?"

– Thich Nhat Hanh

Only you...

My peace, my serenity,
My shadow, my identity,
My night, my fantasy,
My pain, my agony,
It's you, only you...

My thoughts, my loneliness,
My tears, my happiness,
My mischief, my innocence,
My restlessness, my patience,
It's you, only you...

My madness, my obsession,
My love, my devotion,
My silence, my words,
My life, my emotions
It's you, only you...

"Night and day, you are the one."

– Cole Port

Love in life

When life takes an unexpected turn and things don't go your way,
All you want is the pain to go away,
The invisible tears, the agony when you smile,
Makes you wonder, is this really worthwhile?

And when you start feeling there's nothing nice,
Life throws you a big surprise,
You meet "the one", who changes your life around,
A true love, a caring friend, one who makes sure you never feel down.

The miseries turn into hope,
You start smiling more,
Everything changes for the better,
You want these memories to last forever.

Cherish the good things, let go of the pain,
You never know when life takes an unexpected
turn again.

"Cherish every moment with those you love at every stage of your journey."

– Jack Layton

Moments

There are a million things I would like to say,
When I look at you, it just melts away,
The unspoken words, the unseen touch,
makes me feel closer to you so much.
I can feel the aura when you are beside me,
the feeling that you are a part of me.

Your thoughtful eyes, your mischievous smile,
Every moment spent with you is worthwhile
What the future holds for the two of us, I don't know,
But being with you is what I can't let go.

"*We do not remember days; we remember moments.*"
– Cesare Pavese

Love is beautiful

You are my inspiration,
The reason for celebration,
You intrigue me, you challenge me, you make me feel good,
Your belief is what, sees me through.

Life was mundane before you came,
Ever since, it's not the same,
Every morning I wake up with a new hope,
To face everything and not give up.

Every word has a different meaning,
Every song gives a different feeling,
Everything around looks bright and colourful,
You've made me realize, love is beautiful.

"The best and the beautiful things in this world cannot be seen or even heard but must be felt with the heart."
– Helen Keller

A happy you

It's hard for me to see you feel low,
It's even harder for you, I know,
I want to be there for you, when you need me,
I understand I can't fix things, neither can I just let you be,
I want to listen to what you are going through,
I want to take away all the worries from you,
I feel like holding your hands and saying everything's alright,
Inspire you to give it your all and make it right,
I wish I could say the perfect words to make your problems disappear,
Wipe out all the disturbing thoughts and make your mind clear,
See you smiling and laughing as you always do,
All I want is a happy you.

"The most important thing is to enjoy your life – to be happy – it's all that matters."
– Audrey Hepburn

Allow me

Allow me to think about you
every time my heart beats,
Allow me to forget myself,
when our eyes meet,
Allow me to miss you,
reminiscing the time we spent together,
Allow me to love you,
now and forever.

"My love is deep; the more I give to thee, the more I have, both are infinite."

– William Shakespeare

You are the reason

You are the reason I always smile,
You are the reason I run that extra mile,
You are the reason I long to live,
You are the reason I do what I believe,
You are the reason I rise above,
You are the reason I trust in love.

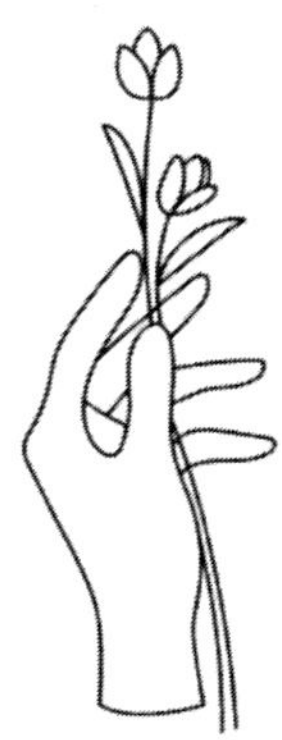

"If I know what love is, it is because of you."
- Hermann Hesse

Take my love

Give me the tears that drown you,
Take all my smiles, it's for you,
Give me the darkness in your life,
Take all the sunshine that's mine,
Give me the thoughts that bring you pain,
Take all my serenity, peace and remain sane,
Give me the hatred that makes you suffer,
Take all the love I have, it's only yours.

"If you have only one smile in you give it to the people you love."
– Maya Angelou

Broken Heart

"It is strange how often a heart must be broken before the years can make it wise."

Sara Teasdale

"The heart was made to be broken."

Oscar Wilde

"The heart will break but broken live on."

Lord Byron

The heart breaks when expectations don't meet reality. It breaks when we lose the ones we love. What remains are memories.

Broken heart

Uneasy nights, endless dreams,
No one to talk to, silent screams,
Paused time, countless thoughts,
Unsure of next steps, totally lost,
Forced laughter, unstoppable tears,
Not able to think straight, everything unclear,
Stressed mind, insecure feelings,
No control on emotions, terrible mood swings,
Empty life, heart full of pain,
With a broken heart, it's difficult to fall in love again.

"Never love with all your heart, it only ends in aching."
– Countee Cullen

Why, dear heart?

Why, dear heart?
Why do you feel so much?
Why do you yearn for a tender touch?
Why do you believe everything is as it seems?
Why do you let go of my dreams?
Why do you fall in love without thinking it's right or wrong?
Why do you give up when you have to stay strong?
Why do you quit when I need you to try?
Why do you pain so much that I want to cry?
Why, oh why, dear heart?
You are a part of me, I can't even tear you apart.

"Courage, dear heart."

– C.S. Lewis

Memories

I'll never forget...

The look of longing in those eyes,
The desire to see me smile,
The comfort of the hands holding mine,
The need to ensure I am fine,
The strength of your arms when I think I'll fall,
The solace of silence but still knowing all,
The quiet understanding that we shared,
The way you showed me that you cared,
The freshness each day as though we had just met,
The one love of my life, I will never forget.

"Memory is the diary we all carry about with us."
– Oscar Wilde

Without you

I look around and there is so much of void,
I extend my hand to feel you beside,
I turn, thinking it's you,
What I see is emptiness all through.

I laugh aloud, replaying the fun times we had,
I knew it would be tough, but not as bad,
There are times I feel so much pain,
All I want is to be with you again.

Missing you has become my favourite pastime,
The silence hurts, nothing seems fine,
Moments we've shared keep coming back again and again,
Without you, things will never ever be the same again.

"If you live to be a hundred, I want to live to be a hundred minus one day so I never have to live without you."

– A. A. Milne

Am I asking for more?

The time that we spent together,
is etched in my heart forever,
The memories, a bag of mixed emotions,
and a heart full of lovely impressions,
An experience that was unforgettable,
A love so pure and unconditional,
Times have changed and so have we,
Instead of us, it is you and me,
The love we have for each other is still the same,
The situation, circumstances are all to blame,
There are so many thoughts we want to share,
We are caught up in our own world with no time to spare,
I know we cannot get back to what is already gone,
I am trying to console myself to just go on,
All I know is I want more of you,
Few seconds of precious time only with you,
When I can look into your eyes and convey what I feel,
Just talking and listening to you without having to conceal,
I want to live through what we shared before,
You need to tell me, am I asking for more?

"The best thing to hold onto in life is each other."
– Audrey Hepburn

Reminiscence

I feel blessed to have been a part of you,
An emotion so beautiful I never knew,
Doesn't matter if it was for a brief time,
Your love will last for a lifetime,
Never had I felt a love so true,
Until end of time, I'll always love you.

"A memory is a beautiful thing, it's almost a desire that you miss."

– Gustave Flaubert

Distance between us

A little indifference, a little push,
Lack of attention, a slight overlook,
Plenty of signs to drive me away,
Creating a distance between us every single day.
I thought we shared everything, there was no mask,
Instead of giving the signs, all you had to was ask,
As there is nothing more than your happiness that matters to me,
You should know by now that I love you more than I love me.

"Never close your lips to those whom you have already opened your heart."

– Charles Dickens

Empty Life

Feeling empty,
Nothing inside me,
Struggling to cope,
I am not me,
Each day just goes by,
Not a thing to look forward to,
Mundane life,
Nothing seems true,
Immersed in work,
Diverting mind,
Losing self,
Life has not been kind,
Responsibilities galore,
Trying to be strong,
No hope of change,
Life goes on,
Sleepless nights,
Pillow full of tears,
Wanting to dream,
There's so much fear,
No one to take care,
I feel the pain,
To live my journey,
I need love again,
I fear though,
This shall not be,
For the rest of my life,
I'll have only me.

"Life is an empty dream."

– Robert Browning

Questions

Where has all the smiles gone?
Where is all the love you had shown?
Where is the happiness I once felt?
Where are the wonderful feelings that were said?

Why is there sadness in my eyes?
Why do I feel I am just going through my life?
Why do present days seem endless?
Why do past days seem priceless?

"Memory is the treasury and guardian of all things."
- Cicero

Going further away

Going further away,
A little everyday,
A little more distant than yesterday,
I can feel you going away.

There's nothing left to say,
There's still a lot to say,
Please don't go away,
I only want you to stay.

"Presence is more than just being there."
– Malcolm Forbes

Look into my eyes

A hundred feelings buried inside,
everything is fine.
A thousand thoughts running through the mind,
there are no signs.
A million words struggling to pour,
there's nothing to say.
Look into my eyes just once,
they'll give everything away.

"Where words are restrained, the eyes often talk a great deal."
– Samuel Richardson

I understand

I understand that you have no time for me,
I understand that I am no longer your priority,
I understand when you choose not to respond to anything,
I understand when you don't tell me everything,
I understand when you don't care about me,
I understand now that you no longer love me.

"Pleasure of love lasts but a moment. Pain of love lasts a lifetime."

- Bette Davis

Hide those eyes

Hide those eyes darling,
They'll spill out the invisible tears,
They'll give away your hidden fears,
They'll reveal the scars you are concealing,
They'll convey the deepest of feelings,
Hide those eyes darling...

"We try to hide our feelings, but we forget that our eyes speak."
- Anonymous

Once upon a time

Once upon a time,
The days were filled with fun,
The heart was with the loved one,
The moment all seemed flawless,
The dreams brought a smile to the face,
Life seemed wonderful and fine,
Once upon a time…

"Sometimes you will never know the value of a moment until it becomes a memory."

– Dr. Seuss

It's all about me

"Be yourself; everyone else is taken."

Oscar Wilde

"Your time is limited, so don't waste it living someone else's life."

Steve jobs

"Always be yourself, express yourself, have faith in yourself, do not go out and look for a successful personality and duplicate it."

Bruce Lee

Our life is ours to decide. It's not selfish, it's important.

It all belongs to me

Every single drop of tear I shed,
Every struggle that is unsaid,
Every dream I see,
It all belongs to me...

Every feeling that is so true,
Every pain I've gone through,
Every emotion that I feel,
It all belongs to me...

Every battle I fight,
Every sleepless night,
Every fear that scares me,
It all belongs to me...

Every memory that leaves me smiling,
Every moment that is inspiring,
No one can take it from me,
It all belongs to me...

"The greatest thing in the world is to know how to belong to oneself."

– Michel de Montaigne

I know

I know I can do it,
Pull myself up from any deep pit,
I know I am strong enough,
To face anything with my chin up,
I know I can manage to smile,
When there are thousand worries inside,
I know I can face things alone,
Life has taught me lessons that were unknown,
I know I am as crazy as it gets,
To do what I believe in, better than regrets,
I know what I am made of,
A bag full of emotions and infinite love,
I know a lot about me,
But every single day I discover a new me.

"Knowing yourself is the beginning of all wisdom."
- Aristotle

It's my life

Let me live my life the way I want,
I have been listening to others, too much, too long,
It's now time to do what I want to,
Live my dreams and make it come true.
I want to live without any inhibitions,
Lead life on my own terms, no conditions,
Do what I trust is right, what makes me strong,
Not rely on anyone to tell me what is right or wrong,
Follow the directions my heart gives,
Change all my miseries into bliss,
I believe I can do this, I have hope in my eyes,
I should listen to myself, after all it's my life.

"Let me live my life the way I want to."
– Jimi Hendrix

I want...

Happy smiles surrounding me,
I want to be a part of it indeed,
Beaming faces, open arms,
I want to melt without missing the chance,
Caring eyes looking at me,
It's everything I want to see,
Loving gestures touching my heart,
It's all I need for my day to start,
This is what I want in my life right now,
Happiness, joy and lots of love.

"Being deeply loved gives you strength; loving deeply gives you courage."

– Lao Tzu

Being strong

Sometimes I am too tired being strong,
Is it because I've been so, for so long?
Sometimes I just want to give up,
It is as if I have lost all hope,
Sometimes I feel like I am breaking down,
I know, I can't, I am not alone.

I feel life has left me with no choice,
I must keep fighting when I want to rejoice,
I wonder how long I'll be able to carry on,
Though I know I should, before everything is gone,
I need to gather all my inner strength and feel better,
As being strong is the only option I have, to keep myself together.

"You never know how strong you are, until being strong is the only choice."

– Bob Marley

Love yourself

Be you,
You'll be judged a million times for being you,
Do what you want,
Family, society, competition will make sure you end up doing what you don't want,
It's your life,
Everyone still wants to jump in and give you their free advice,
Make yourself a priority,
If there's any time left after fulfilling all your responsibilities,
Follow your dreams,
Practicality of life wakes you up leaving you with nightmares and screams,
Love yourself,
When everything else fails, this one thing works well.

"You yourself as much as anybody in the entire universe, deserve your love and affection."

– Buddha

Our World

"In a gentle way, you can shake the world."

Mahatma Gandhi

"We live in a world in which we need to share responsibility. It's easy to say 'It's not my child, not my community, not my world, not my problem.' Then there are those who see the need and respond. I consider those people my heroes."

Fred Rogers

"No matter what people tell you, words and ideas can change the world."

Robin William

"The world as we have created it is a process of our thinking. It cannot be changed without changing our thinking."

Albert Einstein

"As you are, so is the world."

– Ramana Maharishi

The world we live in is beautiful. It is our thoughts, our actions, our participation, our choices that create, modify, revive the world we live in. Each person knowingly or unknowingly is responsible for what happens in the world.

Changing the world begins with us.

This world is a beautiful place

The world is a beautiful place to live in,
And with beautiful people around, it's a blessing,
Each day will bring in more smiles,
No one will have any reason to cry,
Every moment will become a celebration,
There's no hatred, only positive vibration,
This is what each one of us yearn for,
A heavenly place that is easy to explore.

But the reality is different from what we perceive,
We are blinded by our own desires and what we want to achieve,
Selfishness, ego, growth becomes prominent,
Ready to let go of people so that we remain in the forefront,
Goodness, honesty, emotions are all given up,
Whatever the cost we all want to rise up,
We ourselves are destroying the beauty with all our sin,
But we still want the world a beautiful place to live in.

"We can change the world and make it a better place. It is in your hands to make a difference."

– Nelson Mandela

"If you want to change the world, start with yourself."

– Mahatma Gandhi

Be the change

Be the smile you want to see,
Be the love you want to feel,
Be the happiness you want to share,
Be the person you want to care,
Be the light you want to glow,
Be the compassion you want to show,
Be the forgiveness you want to earn,
Be the tolerance you want to adorn,
Be the blessing you want to give,
Be the life you want to live.

"Be the change you wish to see in the world."
– Mahatma Gandhi

Let the world be filled with love

All that happens around us creates thoughts in our mind,
Thoughts that are loving, hateful or kind,
When we nurture these thoughts it grows,
Love, compassion, hatred, it all begins to show,
What is there within us we transmit along the way,
In our words, actions and in everything we say,
And when it is hatred it spreads instantly,
Filling the world with all the despondency,
Instead spread joy, happiness, positivity, love,
That's what the world needs more of now.

"Spread love everywhere you go let no one ever come to you without leaving happier."

– Mother Teresa

Create a new world

Be good, they say,
But being good only makes people use us their way,
Be selfless; think about others, is what we hear,
But when we need someone, they are nowhere near,
Be honest, it's the best policy, motivates the proverb,
Everyone takes it, nobody offers,
Work hard and you'll be successful is the advice we get,
In reality, no one has the time to notice our sweat.

The time we are in today, it's just a race,
Everybody wants to go ahead, else you'll lose the place,
Doesn't matter who you pull down when you go high,
Relation, friendships are let go without a sigh,
Shaking the very basis of what life has taught us,
Making us wonder if we are giving too much.

Whatever happens out there should not change our poise,
How we live our life is our choice,
If we want the world to be a better place,
Then we must stop participating in the race,
When each person thinks and make these changes in their ways,
Then we can create a world where there is harmony everywhere.

"He who lives in harmony with himself lives in harmony with the universe."

– Marcus Aurelius

Thoughts from my diary

Time is money

"Time will take you where you want to go....

YOU decide the time
YOU decide where you want to go"

\`\`\`

"Time and tide wait for none

Neither do opportunities"

*"How we change with time when times changes,
is what sets us apart"*

Heal the world

"All peace and no hatred make the world a beautiful place"

``````````````````````````````````````````````````````````````````````````````

*"Where would the world be today, if instead of a virus, it was love that was spreading.*

*Just imagine."*

``````````````````````````````````````````````````````````````````````````````

Thoughts are things

"Think what you want to become,
to become what you think"

"Break free from the worries in your mind,
What you seek, you shall then find"

"Develop an attitude of gratitude,
be thankful for all that you have
and attract all the good things into your life"

Love "matters"

"Convey your thoughts,
Speak your mind,
Admit your mistakes,
Express your love.

Before it is too late"

When "we" becomes "I"
And "us" becomes "me"
There's nothing left
Between you and me.

Lost
In thoughts,
In dreams,
In past,
In memories,
In love,
In life,

Find me…

\`\`\`

Begin

Flirting, blushing, holding hands, romantic talks, constant messaging #newlove #excitement

Normal conversations, regular updates, caring, understanding #friends #stillcare

Nothing to talk, nothing to share, nothing to care #strangers #loveless

End

``````````````````````````````````````````````````````````````````````````````````````
``````````````````````````````````````````````````````````````````````````````````````

Not able to let go

The moments,
The feelings,
Love,
You…

I dream of you everyday…
Some are happy visions of the past,
Some that I wish don't come true in the future

Hoped for a loving look; nothing
Wanted a comfort hug, nada
Waited for a message, zilch
Finally accepted, it's all over

Listen

"There'll be people and circumstances that'll make you think you can't,
Listen to your inner voice which says YOU CAN"

"There's life beyond work,
There's life beyond home,
A life where I feel free,
A life where I can just be me.